RAISING KINGS

"A MOM'S GUIDE TO RAISING BOYS TO YOUNG MEN"

SHUMON S. HUDSON

RAISING KINGS

"A MOM'S GUIDE TO RAISING BOYS TO YOUNG MEN"

SHUMON S. HUDSON

Legacy Brand Creators
PUBLISHING

Paperback ISBN 979-8-9876202-0-5
eBook ISBN 979-8-9876202-1-2

Editing, Art and Published
by Legacy Brand Creators Publishing, LLC
www.legacybrandcreators.com

Printed in the United States of America

"I have a voice in this world and

it deserves to be heard"

~ Shumon S. Hudson

PREFACE & ACKNOWLEDGEMENTS

I want to first give honor and thanks to God who is the head of my life. Without His love and guidance, I would not be where I am today. I accepted Him at an early age, and I do not regret it one moment as He has helped keep me focused when so much can go wrong around me.

I want to also dedicate this book to a few people who have been there with me every step of the way. I want to thank my mom Tonette Spears for giving me the blueprint of how to be a mom. So many of the lessons that I imparted to my boys were based on how I was reared. I'll be honest, I didn't like it then LOL, but I am forever grateful for it now. I am thankful that as I've grown older, she is not only my mom but also my friend. I love you Ma Dukes!

I want to thank my dad James Spears Sr. for always being the quiet voice in my life. He never really said a lot, but when he did… he meant exactly what he said. He has never judged me, regardless of the situation I found myself in. I will always be a Daddy's Girl! I love you Daddy!

I want to thank my brother James Spears Jr. for always being there. From the time my first son was born to when you slept in my room and was up with him before I could get up, and even now, he will be there when/if any of his nephews or I need him. I am grateful for the bond we share. Not many are blessed with this friendship and sibling love that we share. I would not trade it for anything in the world. I love you, man. I hope I show you as much as I tell you!

I want to thank my young Kings; Lazaire Brown, Jr. (LJ), Preston Brown (P-Diddy), Shumar Brown (Shu-Baby), and Jayshawn Hudson (Shawn) for your support of this book and providing me with the content to be able to write it. I wouldn't be the mom I am today without all of you.

LJ, we practically grew up together. God blessed me with you at the tender age of 20 years old, and we've experienced a lot of things in life together. I pray that it has allowed you to look at life in different ways and made you stronger. I see a lot of myself in you. Your drive, your hustle, your push to make things work. You are confident and headstrong. I smile when I see your dreams being revealed before you. I am thankful for you; you helped save me from myself. I love you, son, and I am proud of the man you are becoming.

Preston, you were born when things were good, not just in life but also in my first marriage with your father. Your quiet nature has tested me as a mom to understand what is going on in your head and how to get you to open up. Know that it is ok to experience pain and confusion, but know we don't dwell in those places. You do things differently, and I respect that. You are my brainiac, my athlete, my quiet storm. I am grateful for how our relationship has grown over the years, and I pray we will continue to grow closer. Keep pushing for your dreams and be confident in who you are and what you bring to the table. I love you and I am proud of the man you are growing into.

Shumar, my youngest King. You were born when there was a lot going on in my life. But I truly believe God blessed me with you so that I would slow down and properly think of my next actions. At the time, things were not good with your father, but you helped me heal through the pain I had experienced. You also tested me as a mom because you were the rambunctious one of the crew, always pushing the envelope, but a Mama's boy still. I wish you saw in yourself the greatness that I see in you. Once you embrace that greatness, the world is yours to take, don't be afraid to step out on faith, because God will carry you to heights greater than you could ever imagine. I love you. I also see the young man you are growing into, and I know that you will be great!

Finally, Jayshawn, you came into my life when I met and fell in love with your dad. You showed me that I still had a lot of love to give. You accepted me as your other mom, and I appreciate your love. I am grateful for the relationship that we were able to build. You are an amazing dad too, and I pray that something you have learned from my motherhood will benefit you as you raise Gigi's Kingston…

The experiences, conversations, and journeys that I've shared with my amazing sons are why this book is possible.

Thank you, God, for your grace and mercy to be who I needed to be for my young Kings.

I must thank my husband, Jesse Hudson III. This man will support me in whatever I put my mind to. He encourages me to be great and celebrates me at each accomplishment. I love this man for loving me beyond what I knew was possible. I admit that

I can be a handful at times, but he handles me with such grace (LOL). Thank you, my love, for not only being my husband, but also my encourager, friend, business partner, confidant, and lover. When God joined us together, he broke the mold!

Last but definitely not the least, I want to thank my cousin Tiffany Fant for pushing me to tell my story. She is an amazing community advocate for our people. Her heart is pure and her intentions genuine. She has always said, "Cuz, you did a great job with those boys. You should be proud. You could help some moms out here!" Well, cuz, here it is! I simply say Thank You, and the stage is awaiting to hear this story.

I am beyond grateful for everyone who has poured into my life in so many ways. I finally dedicate this book to two angels that are looking over me from heaven: my Gramma Mildred Fant and my favorite Auntie Cynthia Stitt. These ladies left immeasurable footprints in my life. Never in a million years could I imagine this life without you both in it. Each time I need encouragement or need to see your faces, you seem to appear at the most opportune times. I know that you are watching over me from heaven and sending down your prayers. I can see the smiles on your faces of how proud you are of me, the laughs of excitement of how much progress I've made, and that I am genuinely happy at this point in my life. I love and miss you both! Know that this is just the beginning! Until we meet again…

TABLE OF CONTENTS

INTRODUCTION

Never in a million years did I dream of or imagine being a single mom. Not just a single mom, but a "boy mom". Many young ladies marry with the intention of rearing their children with their husband. The intimate moments of laughter and seeing your children spend quality time playing with their fathers; that is our fantasy, right? I'm sure that I'm not alone in this. You see, I had my first son at the tender age of 20, when I was still learning who I was as a person; middle son at 23, when I was at the height of my first marriage to their father; and my youngest at 25, when the marriage was going downhill until its eventual downfall. I married again at 35 years old to the love of my life, and added another wonderful son to my family.

I questioned what I was going to do with a house full of boys. What did I know about this life of a single mother, and with boys no less? I am a woman, what could I show them? Teach them? Was I prepared? But God said, "You can do this." And so I pulled up my bootstraps and dug in with my heels to experience a lifetime of laughter, learning, and a love for my boys like no other. Some say I was hard on them. Some say that women can't raise boys to be men. I must disagree with this mindset, because as a mother, you must raise your children to be upstanding citizens in this world to the best of your ability. I do agree that boys need a positive male role model in their lives, and I am grateful that I had my daddy, brother, and now my husband, to be that for them.

I wrote this book to share with you some of the learnings that I've experienced as I was raising my young Kings into the young men they are now. By no means is this book meant to say that this is the only way to do this. I was far from perfect, but I learned to be what they needed, and the outcome has blown my mind. As such, I felt compelled to share with you my successes and failures as I was raising my sons. I pray that this book gives you some encouragement that you can do this!

CHAPTER 1

BOYS HAVE FEELINGS TOO

I was scrolling through my Facebook page and came across a cartoon clip. Humor me for a moment while I set the atmosphere for this topic. In the top picture of this clip, it shows a young boy sitting on a bed with tears streaming down his face while his mom had a belt in her hand while saying, "STOP! I can give you something to cry about!! Boys and men do not cry!!!" The bottom picture shows this same young boy, now a young man, sitting on the bed with his face in his hands, seemingly uninterested while his wife is shouting, "Why can't you just show a tiny bit of emotion!?!" This cartoon hit me like a ton of bricks because I saw myself in the early years of my boys' lives telling them to be quiet, to stop crying, and there is nothing wrong with them. Where did this mentality come from? What are we doing to our young men? We are creating emotionally deficient humans that do not know how to share their feelings and not be ashamed of it. As they began to grow up, I changed my thoughts and the atmosphere that I created for them to be comfortable sharing and dealing with their feelings.

Man is seen to be the "leader" in life, and being a leader presents its own share of challenges. Man tends to carry the weight of the world on his shoulders, and this weight can cause him to break down at times. Is he not supposed to release the hurt, pain, anger, disappointment, and joy that he feels through life's experiences? He is a HUMAN FIRST!

As a mom, I was convicted by seeing their faces when I told them to suck it up and to stop all the crying. I learned how to create a space for them to share their feelings openly and for their feelings to be respected. If they are angry, fearful, tired, upset, hurt, happy, or any other range of emotions, I gave them the freedom to express them. I can tell when something is going on, and I ask them to share it with me regardless of how they think I may react. It was important for me to create a safe space at home to let it out and not be judged. As they are growing into men, they will experience things that they will need to be able to express, so that they don't become angry men.

Angry men lead angry families and tend to be in unsuccessful relationships because their significant other feels that they don't care about them or the situations they experience. While that isn't the case every time, it is a fact that many men have never been told that it's ok to express their feelings. It is a generational curse that I wanted to stop with my family.

If we are truly in tune with our children, we should know when something isn't right or when they are extremely happy about something. This can be used to your advantage to create open non-judgmental conversation with them. Each one of my sons is completely different in the way that they manage their emotions and the way that they communicate. My oldest son has always been open about how he feels about things. As a young child, I could ask him what he was feeling, and he would tell me straight no chaser. As he has gotten older, we have a very close relationship, and we talk about anything and everything. I did, however, have to explain to him that there isn't anything that he couldn't tell me because I could tell he would hold back things so he won't disappoint me. When he is happy, he smiles from ear to ear and has a different energy in his walk.

My middle son is completely different. He isn't as open about his feelings and emotions, and tends to hold things in until he is ready to talk about them. Even when I know that something is going on, I offer my shoulder, ear, and a hug, and let him know that I am available when he is ready. He tends to eventually come around and talk about what is bothering him. It is also hard to tell when he is truly happy about something. His facial expressions don't change a lot and his energy is mild. Nothing seems to get him riled up. He is such a mellow young man, and I have learned to meet him where he is.

He has played football since he was just a little guy, which had become a super important part of his life as he aged into high school. He was the varsity quarterback, and in his junior year, it was the start of an amazing season that would prepare him for college recruitment. But in the third game of the season, he broke his hip and there went his junior year of football. In that moment of the injury, He was in pain, so he cried and I allowed him that space to feel in that moment. But he also wanted to see the team win, so he was energetic and encouraged them to keep on playing. As we received the news from the emergency room physician that he would need surgery and his season was over, and that there was a chance that he would not play again, he cried even more. And he poured all of those tears out from fear and disappointment. In that moment, I felt helpless. I was in the moment with him because I know what football means to him. But he felt that his future in sports was over. The recovery process was even harder as he dealt with watching the team play without him, and he felt that he had let his team down by getting hurt.

We should not assume that since they are boys, they will be fine and they will get over it. We have a responsibility to nurture those feelings and allow them to sort through them, not feeling less than the world says they should be and feel.

My youngest son was my biggest challenge yet. He was a mixture of his brothers. There were times that I could ask him questions and he was an open book, but there were occasions when he knew I was disappointed when he would hold everything in and not say a word. There were many days when it felt as if I was talking to a brick wall. And he was, and still is, a bit stubborn.

I learned to understand him and to tell him that even though I may be disappointed, I still needed an answer to my question. I will be honest—there were days when I laid down punishments for his lack of communication. Am I proud of it? No! Did it work? No, so I had to find another way. I had to begin a conversation and share with him why I needed to know these things. I know, I know. He's a child and I don't need to explain anything to him. Well, he was a child at that time, but as I said in the beginning, every child is different. He still carries some of this trait today in his communication methods.

I was blessed to have a Bonus son to join our family when he was 13 years old. What an instrumental age in a young person's life, especially for a boy, as he is learning who he is as a person— a boy, a young man. When he came to live with us, he was angry, and it showed in his actions. He didn't smile much, and everything was terrible and bad to him. I had to understand that he was joining us from a different rearing, different environment, rules, and life. I had to allow him time to adjust to his new surroundings while encouraging him to stay in close contact with his mother and siblings. He eventually began to mellow out and to fall into the routine of our home.

We are open, loving, laughing, and supportive at all times, but there are rules and discipline that must be abided as well. He has changed and grown so much since he has been with us. He has opened up so much and is ok with processing his feelings and expressing them effectively.

Boys have feelings too and we must not discount that. Wounded boys make wounded men, husbands, and fathers. This is a generational curse that needs to be broken. Learn how your young King operates and processes his feelings, and meet him there until you find the way that he opens up to you. Even though you are a Mom, there may be a trust issue there (that is a topic for another day). Love your young Kings. Validate their feelings and emotions. Allow them to respectfully express themselves and show them how to process their feelings—just like when you have a bad day, get angry or upset. Just because they are young people does not mean that they are not allowed to have a bad day as well. They are human just like you.

CHAPTER 2

HE CAN FEND FOR HIMSELF

Growing up as a young woman, I was taught at an early age to do certain things, such as making my bed each morning after waking, cleaning the kitchen (wash dishes, wipe counters, and sweep the floor) after every meal, keeping my room tidy, and making sure the bathroom stayed presentable along with how to make simple meals so that I or my brother could eat something should we become hungry before our mom returned home from work or before dinner was ready. Now, I had to wonder why all of these things are placed on a young woman to do. Is it so that she doesn't feel that she is depending on a male figure to do these things for her?

I have witnessed moms who cuddle and cod their boys, keeping them from doing such simple chores around the house and in the yard. What are we teaching them about responsibility? In my conversations with other moms, I have heard them admit that their nine- and ten-year old's don't take out the trash, or make up their beds, or help in the yard. I sat in amazement and wondered why these chores were not taught to our boys so that he can fend for himself. What would he do if something happened to you? Can he make at least a simple meal or clean up behind himself? If we place these same expectations on our young men, I do believe that the outcome would be astounding. These boys will rise to the occasion and learn that they CAN fend for themselves.

Having three boys of my own and raising them solo for several years, they began to learn early how to do certain things. Not only did I want them to be self-sufficient, but I wanted them to grow to be great men, and eventually husbands and fathers. Every few years, I would add an additional chore for them to learn. At the age of three to four years old, they had the responsibility of picking up their toys after play time. We would sing the "Clean Up" song and make it fun, and I would walk around with them to show them how to pick up their toys and where they should go. Eventually, when I sang the "Clean Up" song, they knew exactly what to do on their own.

At the age of seven years old, I had them complete simple chores like making their beds each morning with my help or gathering the trash from bedrooms and bathrooms on trash collection day. By the age of nine, they were making up their beds on their own, keeping their rooms clean and vacuumed along with taking the trash can to the corner on trash day. They found great pride in doing these things. As they grew older, the excitement of helping around the house waned, so I had to explain the importance of doing these things. I explained that there was one of me and three of them, and that for us all to be able to do fun things together, we had to take pride and be responsible in our home, which required all our help.

When they began to want to have friends over and to go to different places, I had to remind them that household chores come first. By the age of ten, they were doing their own laundry, washing dishes, cleaning their bathrooms, assisting with spring cleaning, and helping out in the yard. I've heard other moms say, "They don't do it as well as I do, so I will do it myself." What is that teaching them? Show them how you want it done, and if they half do it, you require them to do it again. This became a thing in our home for a little while. My sons would rush through the work just so they could say they did it, and then they would leave with their friends, especially if I was busy or not at home. Once I returned, I would check on the work, and if it was not done correctly, I'd call them to come home to re-do it, and they were not allowed to leave again. A few rounds of this caused this game to stop, and they learned to do it the right way the first time.

The older they got, the more responsibility they gained, until eventually they were learning to cook meals from scratch. They were not just warming up frozen meals in the microwave or making bowls of cereal; they were learning to make vegetables, chicken, macaroni and cheese, etc. They may not enjoy cooking, but they know how to do it, and they do it quite well. I knew there would be a time that they would eventually be on their own, and that time has come. I'm not worried about them depending on someone else to feed them because they can do it themselves, and they actually cook better than many of the young ladies they've dated.

As I look back over these times and the young men that they have grown into with the skills that they've gained, I can say that I'm proud. It makes me smile when I would call and ask them what they are doing, and they would say they are cleaning up or cooking dinner. I love to get their calls on the phone or FaceTime when they are in the grocery store and need a reminder of what to buy when they want to make a meal we've made before or when I walk them through how to cook something they have a taste for.

I am reminded of a time where these teachings were very helpful at their young age. There came a time when I wasn't feeling well, and what they'd learned came into play. As I barely had the energy to lift my head, my oldest said, "Mama, I got it; get some rest." He helped his brothers with their homework, made them something to eat that wasn't microwaved, and made sure everyone had baths and were ready for the next day. He cleaned the kitchen, shut the house down for the night, brought me soup and orange juice, and asked if I was ok. All I could do was cry once he left the room because I knew then that God had given me the strength to do right by them and that I was blessed.

We have a responsibility to teach our young men life skills. They should never HAVE to depend on anyone to do things for them. They should be able to clean, cook, take care of a yard, do laundry and all of the things concerning a home and they should be able to do them well. Start to think about the skills they should know and learn. Create a list and a schedule of how and when you want to introduce them to these different life skills. Your schedule, and not anyone else's, because you know your child best. Do what works for you and your family, but let us not fail them. Not only will it make your load lighter, they will be all the greater for it.

Our young men have this ability, and we must help them realize the greatness within themselves. I promise; they can fend for themselves if we teach them how.

CHAPTER 3

HE IS YOUR SON, NOT YOUR MAN

We tend to either baby our young men or make them mature before their time. There is a happy medium, I promise that it is. Your son should not be privy to everything that is going on with the household bills, your relationships, and anything else that is still beyond his understanding. He is your son, not your man, and he should NOT be expected to fix it. There will be a time that you will be able to share some of these things with him, but that is when he is older, able to digest it, and respect it for what it is. A Lesson… Allow me time to unpack this for you.

We'll all go through hard times. And many times when we find ourselves raising young men on our own, we like to call them the "Man" of the house. BUT HE IS NOT! The man of the house can handle financial responsibility and emotional situations related to a family and the household. But our sons are boys, young men, and they should NOT know the details of the financial situation at home. Why does he need to? He can neither fix nor change it. Now, is it ok to share that you need to cut back in some areas, or you can't buy the new cereal this week, or that particular and expensive pair of shoes for his birthday? Of course, it is! But he doesn't need to know if you are on the verge of the lights being cut off or you and him being evicted because he can't emotionally process what this means, and this can put undue stress on him.

When my son's father initially left the home, he wasn't contributing anything toward our living expenses (mine or the children). At the time, I was not getting child support (that's an entirely different book LOL), so we lived very lean for a while. I sold every piece of furniture in our home except our beds so I could make ends meet. I told the boys that we were re-decorating, and I made the best of it! We had a picnic every night on the living room floor at dinner time. I laid out a blanket and put a fun movie on and we ate, talked, and laughed until bedtime. This was only for a short period of time, but they didn't need to know the extent because they can't handle it. All I wanted was for them to be happy children and do well in school—nothing more and nothing less. I can only imagine the worry they would have dealt with if they knew about something they couldn't fix.

Share with them what is necessary when they notice and ask questions, but be prepared with an age-appropriate answer. They may notice that the cable doesn't have all of the previous channels; explain that you had to make some important decisions and that is one of them. Give them options such as watching movies on Youtube, going outside to play with friends, reading a book, or completing a puzzle, etc that removes their attention from what they don't have while always reminding them to be grateful for what they still have. This is how you keep them in the boy realm. Because he is not a man.

Let's talk about relationships. We are shy about introducing our young girls to someone new in a relationship too early. This should also apply for our boys as well. They deserve that same respect for the same reasons of not introducing too many people in their lives who may not stick around. To protect them from habits that others may harbor and bring around your children, the trust needs to be just as great around our young boys as our young girls. Why? Because by watching you interact with other men, they are learning how they should treat women by how you are treated. You haven't taken the time to know how this man may eventually treat you before you have introduced him to your son. So think about it, sis; what are you teaching him?

Men, even young men, are natural protectors. Don't place your son in the predicament of feeling like he must protect you from a grown man. That is not his responsibility. But you are the Mama, so he is going to protect you at all costs. What if that man hurts your son? Then what? Protect and shield your son like the young king that he is! Allow him to be a child and to grow. Don't throw him out there before he is ready. Every man that you choose to date is not Uncle or Cousin or so and so. Why are we displaying it as a family dynamic? That indicates dysfunction and sets the wrong tone. An Uncle or a Cousin should not be staying overnight with you in your bed. You would only condition your children to believe that this is ok, but it isn't. You are telling them one thing but displaying another.

Your son is not your stand-in date when you are lonely. Yes, I said it. It's harsh but true! If you want to dress him up and take him out to spend time with him, that is ok, and you should do that but for the right reasons and on his terms. If it's a date night, take him to do things that he would enjoy. If not, don't do it. But if he wants to play with his friends and he does not want to go out to dinner with you at a fancy restaurant, don't force him; he won't enjoy himself and neither will you.

As he grows older, he may start relishing those things. That is when he will cherish his one-on-one time with you, experiencing new things and conversation that is an invaluable memory. Take it one step at a time. The day will come when he will enjoy those things and you can introduce him to the finer things in life. Because it is time for him to experience them, not because you want a stand-in date.

Now, I will agree that there are some things that a man does for a woman that they should be shown, taught, and allowed to experience, such as taking out the trash, pumping the gas, cutting the grass, or small projects around the house. However, you are showing him these things as life skills, not because you have deemed or named him the "Man of the House".

CHAPTER 4

CHIVALRY IS NOT DEAD

In my eyes, chivalry is seen as kingly, a way of carrying yourself with the utmost respect. It is treating others the way you want to be treated. It exudes a level of sophistication and grace that matches the height in your spine, the strength in your arms, and the power in each step you take. So, when did it become acceptable for our young people to be poorly dressed, rude, disrespectful, spoiled brats? Yes, I said it because it is true.

Unfortunately, for some of us, our experiences in life caused us to overcompensate for things or experiences that our children had no control over. I'm guilty of overcompensating, but when I realized it, I fixed it! I wanted my children to experience the finer things in life, but I wanted them to be appreciative and to respect the work it took to make these things possible. This comes with manners that many of us were taught as young people. We say, "Yes, ma'am", "No, ma'am", "Yes, sir", "No, sir", "Please", and "Thank you". We address those in a room when we walk in regardless of age, race, or gender. But when did these old school teachings stop being important and taught? I thank my mom for teaching me the manners that I've passed on to my young Kings as I raised them to be men.

There is no better feeling than to hear someone tell you that your children are so respectful and have great manners. I would expect nothing less from them because it was expected in our home. Along with respect and manners comes the art of "CHIVALRY".

Early on, I told my Young Kings that when they walk out of the house, not only do they represent themselves, they represent us as their parents. When you are going to be in public, make sure that you show yourself as presentable. Dress appropriately, face should be clean, your hair done, teeth brushed and sparkling. LOL! It's unfortunate, but people will create their own personal biases based on your initial interaction and appearance. Don't allow people to categorize you with others that are not like you.

At a young age, my Kings opened car doors for me, and held doors for women coming in or out of buildings. Once they were older, I allowed them to open the door for me and I walked in before them. When they were younger, I didn't allow them to walk in after me because I was responsible for their safety. They did, however, still open the door. They loaded groceries into the car at the grocery store, and when we returned home, they unloaded them from the car. If we were in the store, they carried bags from purchases so that my hands could be free. Even once they became teenagers, they became my protectors. They wanted to know where I was going, with who, and they checked in regularly. They watched over me while we were in public places. That is chivalry.

They said "Please" and "Thank you" to anyone they encountered. And to anyone older than them, it was "Yes" and "No, Ma'am", "Yes" and "No, Sir". It was common for them because it was expected at home. They were not allowed to say "Huh" or "What" to an adult at any time. They were corrected immediately, because that to me was a sign of disrespect. If you did not hear or understand what was said, you should say, "Excuse me?" Or ask for the statement or question to be repeated.

I thank my husband for showing them how to "Court" a young woman by the way that he still courts me even after 10 years of marriage. He's thoughtful in every interaction. He talks to me kindly even when he is upset. He is hands-on with the things I need help with. He doesn't want me to do hard hands-on projects, but he doesn't stifle my desire to do so. He opens the car and building doors. He waits to eat until my food arrives. He holds my hand and shows me that he cares. He opens doors for women who are carrying children, and he offers his assistance where possible. My young Kings follow these things because of what they have seen in our home, what they've been taught about treating other people.

It is ok to be kind to a fellow human being. We must get back to teaching our children the value of manners and respect. You can be bold and still be humble. Begin at a young age and teach them life skills that will carry them far. At each stage in life, they should learn something new that will mold them into the adults that they will eventually become. Once they leave the nest, you can't control what they do, but you can count on the fact that what you've taught will stick with them. A situation will appear at some point, when they will remember how to put these learnings to good use.

CHAPTER 5

IT'S OK TO BE CONFUSED

When you were blessed with the gift of being a mother, whether it was planned or not, I'm sure there were a variety of emotions that you felt. Excitement, fear, confusion, the list goes on. Why? Because you were embarking upon a place you have never been before; unchartered territories. Sure, you could look at how you were raised and emulate or not those actions and experiences. You could look at how friends were raised or how they are currently raising their children and borrow some of the things that you see and incorporate it into how you rear your own child. But, in all honesty, there is a big question mark that looms over your head each day: Am I doing this right? Is this ok to do? Am I hurting my child's feelings? Yes, and the questions could go on and on. But the reality is that there is not a book out there that can tell you step by step how to raise your child. If there was, just know that there is no one-size-fits-all when it comes to parenting. Your style will be represented by a variety of factors, including your upbringing, today's society, and the child themselves. You will adjust based on the best needs for each child. It is ok to be confused on what to do. Let's also add the fact that you are raising Kings, and you, my dear, are a woman. Their needs are a bit different.

As my children began to grow, I learned so much about being a "boy mom". They wrestled with one another and wanted to play football in the house, and at the same time wanted to cuddle beside me and watch movies. I learned to go with the flow and to give them what they needed. I may not understand it, but they needed it and it was my responsibility to give it to them. As they grew older, their personalities began to blossom. They were either very outgoing or very introverted, and I had to learn how to manage both of these. I am a very extraverted, outgoing person, so I couldn't understand why 2 of my sons were not this way. Where did this come from? I began to question myself on my parenting style. Did I make them feel as if their voices weren't heard? Were they being bullied at school? Was I not giving them enough attention? I learned it was none of these things. They just chose to be this way. They had their select group of friends and I learned to manage the 2 that didn't really hang out socially with the 2 that always had a packed calendar of events. Woe is me!

It was important for me to work with each child individually to understand their needs. As they reached puberty, things became even more confusing. The mood swings (YES, boys have them too), the long showers with LOUD music, always wanting to stay in their room, not wanting to be a part of family gatherings. I learned it was a part of them becoming who they are as individuals. Just as adults need me time to figure things out, so do children. It is also important to engage their minds and to understand what they are watching, listening to, who they are talking to, and what is going on in their world. You will continue to be confused if you are not a part of their world.

The next phase had them always wanting to be home and to have their friends over. I didn't understand why they wanted to be at our home all the time. Then I learned that they felt safe here and their friends enjoyed being here with us. I gave them their space, but I also included myself into their conversations. They thought I was the cool mom, even though they knew there were rules and expectations when you stayed at our home. This gave me an opportunity to learn more about my sons and how they interacted with their friends. This shed a lot of light for me as I watched them grow into men.

Here comes the dating phase (OMG)! They are so kind, gentle, loving, and chivalrous! All I could do was smile because I was watching what they have been taught play out like a movie before my very eyes. But, I also saw that they were so loving that they failed to see some things that these young women were doing right before their eyes. I was conflicted on whether I should say something or let them learn on their own. What attracted him to her? What does she bring to the table? What is her family like? Why does he act this way after being around her? I was sooo confused until I finally sat them down and had a conversation about what I was witnessing. I had to also understand that this is new, and they are learning, but they need to also be aware that I am watching and I want what is best for them.

So, mom, it is ok to be confused. It is ok to not have all of the answers. It is ok to tell them you don't know. Just know that they need you there in so many ways and that you are learning and growing together. One day, it will all make sense.

CHAPTER 6

BE CONFIDENT BUT RESPECTFUL

Our young Kings have been dealt an interesting hand in life: they are seen as a threat at a very early age. Their beautiful brown skin makes people uncomfortable for reasons I have yet to understand. So many of them are reared without their fathers in their lives, or the men in their lives are not being there consistently, or worse, even if they are there, the example they are showing may not have been positive. But Moms, you can still rear a strong, confident King.

One thing that used to bother me is that they would walk with their heads down. I stopped that immediately! Why is your head down? What are you looking down at? You can't see where you are going, what is in front of you, or prepare for what is to come if your head is always down. Lift your crown, young King. Look forward, look up so that the sun can bring about a glow to your beautiful brown skin. Look up to the SON so that he can give you guidance and direction.

Stand up straight and look people in the eye when you are speaking with them, and greet them with a strong handshake. The strong handshake and that direct eye contact projects poise, confidence, and demands respect. Any time you are speaking with someone young or old, you give them the same respect that you expect to receive. I've always shared with them that they may not like you, but they will respect you. Carry that everywhere you go!

As my sons were growing, there were times when there were disagreements with adults on a variety of topics. They were always taught it is ok to disagree but to do it respectfully. You can say what you want or need to say and not be disrespectful. It is not always about what you say; it is more about how you say it. Come to the table humbly with why you disagree, and show and prove it. This shows that you have taken the time to think through your response and not simply acting out of anger, deceit, and frustration. Be confident in what you believe in. If someone can easily talk you out of what you believe in or easily talk you into something that you don't believe in, where is your respect for yourself?

Always carry yourself with grace. Be particular about your appearance. You don't have to look like everyone else! But your style should be one of class and dignity. Give people a reason to want to connect with you. Don't be cocky, even if you know the answer or you feel that yours is the best. Be open to hearing from others because you may learn something; remember, we don't know it all in any topic. At times, your confidence will be seen as arrogance, but that is okay. That is not your issue to address. If your presence intimidates them, that is a personal issue that they must deal with internally. You set the bar and let others join you there. You don't dumb down to what they are doing and saying, and this applies to anything.

Teach your King that it is ok to be good but expect to be great! Don't settle for the status quo. Try your hand at many things so that you are well-rounded and can speak confidently in conversations. And when you don't know anything, be even more confident in admitting that you don't know while being committed to finding the answer. There is no glory in overworking yourself because your mental health is more important than anything. However, when you are dedicated to something, know that while you are sleeping, someone else is working. Make the best out of the hours that you do have. Work smart, not hard, and be GREAT at it!

CHAPTER 7

HE WANTS YOU THERE

You may not know anything about his interests. It could be cars, sports, music, or anything else. But if it is important to him, it should be important to you. You won't be a master of his interests and it isn't your responsibility to be, but you should know enough to show that you are interested, that you can have a conversation with him and that you care about his interests.

My middle son was very interested and involved in golf in his younger years. I thought it was the most boring thing in the world that he could take up interest in, but I asked questions, found him a trainer, bought him golf clubs, took him to practice his craft, and even sat through a few matches just to be there. Why? Because even though he may not say it, he wants you there.

He wants your approval; he wants to hear you cheering him on. He may not NEED you there, but he wants you there.

There is no better feeling than seeing your child take the field, court, or stage, where you can tell that they are searching the crowd for your face or tuning their ear to pick up your voice. I was never really into sports until I became a mom. My boys played golf, baseball, soccer, basketball, football, ran track—the list goes on. I made it a point to be there to support them regardless if I knew anything about it or not. Just know that by being there and being an active supportive participant, you can learn a LOT.

There were days when I worked late and I couldn't make the game, and to hear them tell me they missed me being there sparked something different in me. So, even when I traveled for work, there have been days that I left the airport still in my work attire and headed straight to the school for a sporting event, and I made sure to catch their eye when I arrived. The smile on their faces made it worth it! They didn't have to look for me in the stands because I was always in the center with my loud voice, big proud smile, signs, bells, and anything else that would let them know that I am rooting them on. As they get older, they will give the impression that it doesn't matter whether you are there or not. But that is not true. They still want you there!

Even when it isn't sports-related, they want you there as a listening ear or as their security blanket. Even though my young Kings have grown, they still need to know that their mom is there, and that their mom has their back. I receive calls or text on a regular basis from my sons wanting to know what I think about this or that. Mom, they want to know that they can talk to you about anything without judgement. They also still come and lay next to me on the sofa to feel that security and safety. Although your son may not ever tell you that he wants you there, you have to make it a point to be there for him, listen to him, and quietly support him in whatever way works for him. Trust me, there is a sense of trust in just being there!

CHAPTER 8

PERSPECTIVE;
MOM VS. WOMAN; YOU CHOOSE

It was very important for me to have a strong relationship with my sons for several reasons. At the tender age of eighteen, the world already sees them as men. Should they know a lot about the world and the people in it through life experiences? Yes. But do they know enough for us to relinquish them to a world that does not care about their heart or soul? No, our young Kings need us to continue to be there for them throughout this rough world that sees them as an immediate threat. We must continue to show them the way through our learnings and teachings that help them to be better and grow wiser. Experience is a good teacher, but it can be a rough lesson.

At a certain age, young men pick up the Alpha male trait. In our society, it is described as "smelling themselves". This just means that they are beginning to take their place in manhood, and they see themselves as a leader or having a level of authority. This is good as this is a part of the progression of growth, but this can also be a challenge for moms because they seem to believe they have all of the answers. And there will be a time when you can no longer just give them the answer to a question. You must give him the skills to make appropriate decisions for himself. For my boys, this started at different ages depending on their level of maturity. But for the majority of them, it was at the age of eighteen.

I remember very clearly the day that my son came to me and asked me my opinion about a relationship situation. I clearly said to him, "Son, you are at the age now where it is important for you to know that when you ask for my opinion, there are two sides to it. There is an opinion as your mom, and there is an opinion as a woman. Many times, these thoughts won't be the same. Why? Because my answer as mom is to protect you, but before I was a mom, I was a woman first, and I can't ignore how I would feel if

I was in her shoes. I am going to share both with you, then you must decide what to do." Of course, he looked at me like I was crazy and asked why I had to make it so difficult (LOL). But it was time for him to use his reasoning and decision-making skills. I was not in the relationship; he was. So, I began to give him my opinion as a mom first, sharing with him how I viewed her and him when they interacted with one another. I shared the red flags that I picked up upon the initial meeting and being in the same space with her. I shared how I felt that she may be a good person, but I didn't think that she was the best for him. Now, from a woman's perspective, I shared that he could do more as he was raised to be chivalrous, that he was catering a bit too much but it wasn't reciprocated. And as a woman, I would never be in a relationship that was one-sided. I shared with him that if certain things were said or done, I would leave the relationship. I ended this conversation with, "Now you take from this what you feel is important, and you make the decision that is best for you. I will not make the decision for you because you know how you feel, and you know what you want."

As a mom, we must give them the tools for effective reasoning and decision making. Not just in relationships, but in so many other situations as well. You won't always be around to give your perspective, but they will think back on these conversations and use the skills that they have learned through your teachings. We don't realize what we are teaching them through conversation and by just being there in their informative years. These years set the foundation for how they carry themselves and respond to things when life places them at a crossroad.

It is a blessing to see this play out in front of you or to hear them call you and explain a situation that they were faced with, and they share how they reverted to something you said or did that helped them make the best decision. Encourage him and praise him for making a decision that serves him because his mental stability, heart, and soul are so much more important than anyone else's. You must personally be whole before you can offer anything to anyone else.

Continue to have those conversations, but make sure to add two perspectives. And if you aren't having these conversations, make sure that you do. They will thank you for it later because they only see things through their lenses, and not yours as experienced, adult, and a woman. If they have an adult male in their life, include them and ask them to give their perspective. It will also help them to see a responsible male and hear how they would handle a situation or what their thoughts are. Yes, as a woman you can raise great men, but you are not a man and there are things they need to hear from them.

CHAPTER 9

WOULD YOU CHOOSE HIM
AS YOUR HUSBAND?

Now, take a moment to think about the years of your teachings to your son. Have you taught him everything you want him to know? Of course not. We are not perfect, and there is not a perfect guide on child-rearing. You can only strive to do and be your best for them so that they can be the best person in this society.

For me, I did things this way because I was insistent on raising young men that would be a positive and successful addition to this society—as a citizen, brother, friend, and prayerfully eventually husband and father. But above all, I raised them to see themselves as the Kings that they are. They were born with a purpose, and I want to see them fulfill this purpose.

What did you teach your son about being a man? Hopefully, many of the same things that a young girl is taught because the core is the same. Did you raise a dependent, lazy, young man that doesn't know how to do anything for himself and who depends on you for everything?

Did you teach him that cleanliness is next to Godliness or is he a nasty, non-housekeeping slob? Did you teach him to change his sheets weekly, to wipe baseboards on a regular basis, to not leave stains in the tub, toilet, or around the toilet should they miss some? LOL! Does he know that cleaning the kitchen means more than loading the dishwasher? Does he keep his personal space tidy on a regular basis? If you met a man that you were considering spending your life with and he had this nasty quality, would you want to make him your husband?

Did you teach him to be chivalrous? To treat the woman that he wants to be in his life as the queen that she was born to be? Was he taught to open doors, walk on the side closest to the street, to let her walk ahead of him inside of a building, to help bring in the groceries, to bring flowers, and leave small notes of encouragement? The list goes on. These things are important for a lifetime of happiness in a relationship. If you were looking for a man to spend your life with and your son was presented before you, would you choose him as your husband?

Did you show him how to cook? How to prepare even one meal so that he can feed himself if needed? Not a sandwich, not scrambled eggs, not a microwave meal, but to actually bring out the pots and pans with mixing bowls to make a full meal. Even if not for himself, there will be a time when those skills can come in handy. If he is in a relationship, she may not feel well or may be too tired to cook and will need to lean on him to help with dinner. Can he do that without depending on her? When you are looking at the qualities important in a lifelong mate, does your son have this? Would you choose him as your husband?

Is he a spoiled brat and gets upset when everything does not go his way? Have you taught him how to manage his feelings and emotions? How to walk away and be by himself if needed before approaching a situation? Does he know how to speak up when necessary to voice his opinion respectfully and not show off, making himself look like a fool?

Does he know how to care for a lawn? There will be a time that he will be a homeowner, and he will need to understand how to protect his investment. That curb appeal is important because people will automatically make assumptions about the inside of your home based on what it looks like on the outside. Does he know how to use small tools like screwdrivers and hammers and the like so that if he needs to fix something minor, he can save his money and do it himself?

Are you raising a manly man or are you raising a man that depends on everyone but himself? Our young Kings have a charge to keep, and it is first to themselves. They must set standards in every area of their lives or they will fail at anything. It is unfortunate that the world is not putting more support behind them. But what matters is that you are showing him how to carry himself in a society that expects him to fail. Failure is NOT an option!

EPILOGUE

FROM THE HEARTS OF MY SONS:
MY YOUNG KINGS

LAZAIRE JR.

I am Lazaire Jr., I am 26 years old, and the oldest son born to my mom. I am a recent college graduate and building a life of my own in a different state. My mom was only twenty years old when I came into the world. So, you can say that we grew up together. I was the test of many of the parenting skills that have been passed onto my brothers, but I wouldn't change it for the world. It taught me how to handle myself, to be independent but also loving. I consider my mom my road dog, my best friend. Although I have plenty of friends, my mom has been there with me through thick and thin, never judging, always supporting, always a listening ear, and sometimes giving advice that I didn't want but I needed. I know I can count on her to be there when I need her most. She let me grow up, but she always made sure I knew where my home is and that I am always welcome there.

There is so much that I have learned from my mom in watching how she operates daily. She is such a hard worker! She is always striving for more, not trying to get around situations but working through them, and always looking for ways to leave a legacy for us. I watched her be a single mom, work full time, take care of us (cooking, cleaning, chauffeuring us around), and get her degree at the same time. I then watched her show us what love in a healthy relationship looked like when she met and married my Pops. She made it look easy, but I know she worked hard to make that dream a reality for herself. By seeing her do this, it gave me the drive to be successful, go after my dreams, stand on my own two feet, and be confident in who I am. I wouldn't be the man I am today without my mom. She has always encouraged me to keep going, to push the envelope, to be bold but humble, and to use the gifts God has given me to achieve my highest potential. There has never been anything I wanted to do that was good for me that she has not encouraged me to go after. That is why I am in Texas now. Although I know she wishes I were closer, she sees my dream and only wants what's best for me: the one that will make me happy and successful.

My mom has such a big heart and she has accepted my friends as her own. They really appreciated spending time with our family because she loved them, fed them, and talked to them the same way she talked to us. And they learned so much from her just like I did. Although she is Mom, she laughed and joked with us as well, allowing us to be ourselves and in our element.

To this day, my friends always ask about her, how she is doing, how life is treating her. That means a lot to me because many of my friends didn't have this environment at their own home, and they were able to get a sense of what a true family life is when they were with us. She was fun, but there was structure. Me and my brothers knew that, and our friends definitely knew this as well. And I know that is where I get my big heart and genuineness from. I have a heart for people, and I try to be there for them when I can.

Did I already mention that this lady can cook? I love coming home to a home-cooked meal because it is always seasoned to perfection. My mom taught me this very necessary life skill, and I must say I do it quite well (I cook better than any of the women I've dated so far. Thanks Mom! LOL)! She made sure that we could prepare a good home-cooked meal for ourselves and not have to spend extra money eating out or to depend on anyone else to do it for us. I know that if I want a meal, I can go in the kitchen and prepare it myself. We started that at a young age, helping in the kitchen at least once a week. And before we left the nest, she made sure we could recite certain recipes.

In our home, cleanliness was next to Godliness, and she did not play about a clean home and a manicured yard. We made our beds every day, did our own laundry once a week, and cleaned bathrooms, baseboards, cut grass, edged, etc. When it came to taking care of a home, she taught us and made sure that we did it right. We may not enjoy doing these things, but we can never say that we don't know how to do it. I didn't like it at all back then, but truly appreciate it now.

She showed me how to care for myself. You work hard everyday and you make sure that your bills and responsibilities are taken care of, but you must also treat yourself. Life is not meant to just pay bills; life is meant for living. I watched her take care of responsibilities, but I also watched her make sure that she kept her appearance up. She kept her nails and hair done, she dressed nice, presentable, and classy. She definitely passed that on to me. She explained that you only get one time to make a first impression and that it should be the best impression. She always kept us clean, dressed nicely with a fresh haircut, and when we were old enough to appreciate it, we got manicures and pedicures. Her thing was that when you walk out of this house, not only do you represent yourself, but you represent your parents and family too. You don't want people to get the wrong impression of you. I keep these practices to this day. I ensure that I always put my best foot forward.

She taught me how to treat a woman by hearing her, understanding love languages, and being there. Sometimes she feels I am there for them too much, but I digress. LOL! When it is time for me to settle down with the woman of my choice, she truly has some big shoes to fill. I will definitely be looking for someone with similar characteristics as my mom: a loving nature, personality, style, grace, beauty, and love. Someone who can bring peace to our home; a supporter, motivator, great cook, loves God, and a role model to our future children. A tall order, I know, but my mom has set the standard for what I look for in a woman. I am confident when it is time that God will send her to me.

Thank you, mom, for raising me to be the strong, independent, God-fearing man that I am today. I know it wasn't always easy, but you never gave up on me, on us, and you are still here to this day, supporting and motivating us to be GREAT! The good and bad times that we experienced groomed me to be a great man. I know that I am a King because you raised me to be just that! I didn't realize all that she has done for me and us until I truly sat down to think about it. She is still teaching me things even today, and I appreciate her still being so active in my life even as an adult man. So many don't have their mom in that capacity at this age. She has been my everything, and all I want to do is be successful so that I can at least share back with her what she has given me. I love you so much!

PRESTON

Hello to every eye reading this at this moment. My name is Preston Brown, the middle child of four. I am 22 years old and currently playing college football. I'm going into my senior year to earn my degree in Communication studies.

Being the middle child of four was tough for someone like me because it's normal for younger and older brothers to get more attention. Being that I am a closed-off individual, I tend to keep things to myself. Building a relationship with my mom wasn't the easiest thing to do, either. As a young child, I was very sensitive, and oftentimes, I would become upset and cry for reasons that I cannot explain. My mom would try her absolute best to get me to speak, but I could never tell her what was wrong. That was the thing, though; she always tried to help me figure out what was wrong and did everything she could to help fix that. As that young child, I might not have opened up at the time, but to know she was always there meant a lot to me. It built the foundation of our relationship and has drawn me closer to her as I grew older.

Now that I'm 22 years old, I can say that me and my mom have an open relationship. I talk to her as much as she talks to me, and we talk about anything and everything during our conversations. I can call her to ask absolutely anything, and she'll sit back and be the listening ear that I need. I thank her so much for that, and looking back, I appreciate all those times she fought to build a mother-and-son relationship between us.

There are so many lessons that I could say I've been taught, but there are a few that stick out to me. Firstly, I will say the quote she taught us: "It's ok to be good, but I EXPECT you to be great." The quote has stuck with me in everything I do because I know to hold myself to a higher standard. No matter what that task may be, whether that is cleaning up my room or getting more reps when working out on the field or in the gym, I know I have to hold myself to a higher standard, and that my mom also expects that out of me every time. It honestly taught me how to work harder than others around me and approach every challenge, knowing that I can and will dominate it every time.

Additionally, my mom has shown me how to live on my own, and that was something I didn't notice until I moved out for college. I didn't realize that a lot of young adults don't know how to clean up after themselves. My mom made us clean our bathroom, clean up our own room, clean dishes, and do our own laundry as soon as we were of age. I didn't know how important doing these tasks would come in handy after I moved out. Once I did, I was able to see for myself that there are young adults in the world that had their mommies and daddies do all the chores. You go into their rooms and see the filth and understand why our mom didn't let us leave until our chores were done, and done correctly. Furthermore, I was taught how to be a gentleman to women. I was taught how to treat a woman respectfully, such as holding doors, never putting hands on them, and knowing how to talk to them. Holding the door for any woman walking through before you enter yourself is a sign of respect and shows that you know how to be respectful. Never putting your hands on a woman should be a given, but sadly, not to some. No matter how tough the situation gets, never put your hands on a woman. If it gets that tough, be smart and walk away. The aftermath never ends in the man's favor anyways, and as a man, you can physically do more harm than she will. While talking to any woman, you should always show respect. She is not your "bro" or "bruh", and you shouldn't talk to them in that manner. It's disrespectful and looks bad on you as a man because you obviously have no respect for women. My mom made sure that me and my brothers knew these rules as she knew they would be important as we grew older.

I could go on and on about all of the lessons my mom taught me, and I have stories to go along with them. My mom is a superhero to me because the older I get, the more I realize all she has done and still does for us. Being a single mom, raising three black men to not be another statistic on the street is a true challenge. Not only did she do it, but she did it with class and made it seem so effortless. There were rough times, of course, and those were hard times. But my mom always gave me comfort that everything will be alright. She always pushed through, and I know that's where I get it from with the adversity I've faced in my own life.

My mom means so much to me, and I just want her to know that nothing she has taught me was ever taken for granted. She's done so much for me that there isn't enough money in the world to repay her. I just want to be a living example of everything she has raised us to be. I plan to reach success mentally, physically, and financially through the core values and principles she has instilled in me. Like momma always says, "It's ok to be good, but I EXPECT you to be great," and I won't stop until I obtain everything I work for.

SHUMAR

I am Shumar, the youngest of this crew of four, and I am currently 20 years old. The relationship I have with my mom is like two peas in a pod. It reminds me a lot of a childhood cartoon called Beavis and Butthead. One minute we are the best of friends, and the next we are each other's worst enemy because we act so much alike. That is why I call her my twin, besides the fact that we have the same face. LOL!

I was the Momma's boy out of the bunch, so I was always around my mom any chance I could get. If she was about to cook, 9 times out of 10, I was there right beside her helping. That is how I learned to cook. She taught me this life skill that will carry me the rest of my life. I actually enjoy cooking and I'm really good at it, if I must say so myself (ask about me LOL).

If she was going to the store, 9 times out of 10, I was in that passenger seat ready to ask for everything I saw in the store. And I went with her because I knew I would get everything. She was my movie buddy before I realized my brothers were actually cool and not just a bunch of bullies that messed with me because I was the baby. My mom is who I would spend my time with most of the time. She always made me feel welcome, loved, and never a bother to her, no matter what I was doing, and I just know that's where my big heart comes from.

I've had a great experience being raised by my mom. She is always there and caring for me and my brothers through any situation. Even though I say she doesn't, she spoils all of us so much. I can't even front anymore. She made sure all of our needs were met and we were blessed with most of our wants. We had so many more experiences than many of our friends. She taught me everything she possibly could. She knows so much! Even things most women wouldn't know. She was always fixing stuff around the house, taking care of the lawn, preparing full home-cooked meals for us. Now one thing she did not play about was CLEANING! She didn't play about that at all! We may not like to do it, but she made sure we knew how to do our laundry, clean the kitchen, our bathroom, wipe baseboards, and the list goes on! She always said that cleanliness is next to Godliness! Most importantly, she taught me how to treat and cater to a woman. She stood very firm with me and my brothers about that, and that's why we can't keep the ladies off of us LOL! And now I'm going to share with you three things that stuck with me from all that she has taught us.

She always told me that nothing in life is free and to not *EXPECT* handouts or anything. Don't think that somebody is just going to give you something without wanting something in return, or that something is free. You have to go get it for yourself and work for it so you know that it's yours for sure. Anything you work hard for and put your blood, sweat, and tears into, you respect it more and no one can take it away from you.

"IT'S OK TO BE GOOD BUT EXPECT TO BE GREAT!" This is my favorite one. It didn't mean so much to me then because as a kid, I was just doing what I wanted to do without thinking about the outcome. Now, I can truly understand what she meant when she told us this. It means that for anything you do in life, you need to always prepare yourself and expect that you will do great and have a good outcome. It means that while you are being "good", someone else is working hard to be "GREAT". Only you can decide how you measure up against the competition. Never settle for the mediocre level and just be good; always go for great. Think of the rewards of your hard work.

She also taught us to make the best of any situation. My mom always made sure that me and my brothers were taken care of through all the adversity and situations she went through. She never let us see the bad side of it. Now that I am older, she has shared stories with me about how we were almost living in poverty. I was so shocked and surprised I never noticed any of it as a kid. Every night felt like we were eating five-star meals and we were watching movies on the big screen even though it wasn't that; she made it feel that way, and that goes in with making the best of every situation.

I go through a lot now, and I know everybody does, but I try my hardest every time to make the best out of my situation. Hearing what my mother had to go through with three boys by herself, she took it chin up, chest out, and made away, so now I have no excuses but to do just that. I love you, Mama! Thank you for teaching me how to be a Man, a Young King! I'm still growing and I know I will make you proud!

JAYSHAWN

I first met this beautiful lady that I call Momma in the Summer of 2010 when I moved to Charlotte to live with my dad. At 13 years old, I didn't know what to expect, although I knew it would be different. My first one-on-one experience with her was when she took me to enroll in middle school here in Charlotte. When we left the school, I was angry because they told me that I would have to repeat my grade. My attitude was bad that day, and I wasn't talking to anyone. She stood me in front of the mirror, my lips poking out, huffing and puffing, and told me to look at myself. She asked me what I was mad at. Who helped me get to where I was in my education? She made me recognize that no one was responsible for that but me. She then told me that we can overcome this, but I had to put in the work, and she would help me get there. I knew then that she had my back and that things were going to be alright!

My mother is definitely a guide to how I lead and live my life. She taught me the importance of necessities and not wasting money on things that I don't need until I could afford to do so. Now that I am a dad, these teachings come in handy. I remember one day, she sat me and my brother down at the table. She laid out all of the household bills, and then showed us a copy of her and my dad's paycheck. She then gave us both a calculator and made us do the math of what we had coming in financially, what we had going out, and how the frivolous things we were asking for didn't fit in the budget. I was more mindful then about what I asked for. Now don't get me wrong; we were spoiled, but it had to make sense for the household.

It was impressive how she moves around a house full of males. You must have a LOT of patience! She was the only woman in the house with my dad, me, and my three brothers. She had to have a lot of patience with me because I came from a different upbringing until I came here. And not only that… I'm the clown of the bunch LOL! That's love because I know I can get on her last nerves. But through it all, she made sure that we learned how to be men by teaching us skills that will last a lifetime.

My mom can COOK! I love to stop by and see if there are leftovers in the refrigerator. It also gives me more time to spend with her. She is so funny; I am guaranteed a laugh around her. I call her when I need that recipe for my favorite dish she makes. I cook because of her. You know, a man needs to be able to feed himself and not depend on anyone else to do it for him. In fact, I found that I am a better cook than some of the girls that I've dated because of her teaching us this life skill.

I was required to wash my own clothes, and momma taught me how to do that. I had to separate the whites and use Clorox, then separate the darks (nothing red) to make sure our clothes were clean. The girls at school used to like to sniff our clothes because they said we smelled so fresh and clean. I will say that also pushed me to make sure that my laundry was freshly done. LOL! She did not do our laundry for us; we had an assigned day to do our laundry and if we missed it, we were out of luck. So hopefully, you have enough clean clothes to last you until your day comes around again. LOL! She didn't play with us, but it taught us to not procrastinate when handling business. It taught me that everything can't be done on my time, and there are guidelines to follow in every situation.

She pushed me beyond my fears in a few ways. She taught me how to drive by putting me in the biggest vehicle we owned:

the Suburban. No one wanted to drive that big truck, but she told us that if I can drive this, then I can drive. Until I learn to drive this, I won't drive any other vehicle at this house. That is partially why I drive big trucks today! She also pushed me beyond fears academically. In my junior year of high school, I decided that I wanted to graduate on time with my brother. We sat down with the school counselor, and we devised a plan. I would take all of my junior year classes in the first semester and all of the remaining senior year classes in the second semester. I was nervous about this because I knew it was going to be a lot of work, but she believed in me and helped me believe in myself. I was able to work past this fear and graduate on time. I even went on to college, an accomplishment that I didn't think I would ever see if I had not come to Charlotte. I know now that I can do anything that I put my mind into.

Lastly, she taught me how to treat a woman and how to love. The proper way of dating and being in tune with my thoughts and feelings as a man. We were not allowed to talk to or treat young ladies in any way but respectfully. She made sure of that! But she also taught me to not be ashamed of being human and having feelings. She reminded us that just because I was a man didn't mean that I didn't have feelings and that they should be respected and regarded as well.

A good woman like my momma deserves more than what I can give, but as a son, I thank her for showing me the ropes of life. Seeing her in good and bad times as a great mother, wife, sister, auntie, and daughter, but always pushing us to greatness. I hope one day I can enjoy a woman like my momma by my side at the altar.

Thank you, momma! I love you!

You Can Do This!

I am grateful for my sons. I know they talked about how I helped them, but they have no idea how they have helped me. They have taught me so many lessons being their mom. I have laughed, cried, prayed, and prayed some more, but Thanks be to God that we made it through. I am so very proud of the young men they are growing into, each one taking their own path, learning life lessons, and excelling at each turn. My boys are now Young Kings and I am grateful to place the crown on each of their heads to pass on the legacy to their own.

Moms, I know sometimes it feels like you are on your own in this journey. Understand that you are not alone and there are so many that are on this journey with you. Take the time to really get to know your young Kings, delve into their interests, their thoughts, and encourage them to be their best. Pour into them all of the things that you know they should and can be. You will not always get it right and you will not always be liked by them for the decisions that you make on their behalf, but they will appreciate and love you the more for it once they realize how it has benefited them as they grow older.

To the young Kings, if you are reading this book, be kind, be patient, be understanding, and be open to learning. Know that you may not enjoy all that you are being taught, but these things will benefit you as you grow older. Be bold but be humble and let the world experience your greatness! Be the change that the world needs to see through your actions and the energy that you possess. You are powerful in your own right, but you must use power purposefully. You can do this. You are a Young King.

79

KINGS

Keep your Integrity and Never Give your Soul

MEET THE AUTHORS

SHUMON S. HUDSON

'Life doesn't come with a manual,
it comes with a Mother.'

Shumon Hudson is proof that a harmonious relationship between ambition and joy exists. She's discovered the sweet spot of being a dedicated wife and mom of four sons while chasing her dreams as a successful business woman, seasoned artist and entrepreneur.

She is a Healthcare Reimbursement and Market Access Expert in the biopharmaceutical industry. She obtained her Bachelor's degree in Healthcare Administration and a Master's Degree in Organizational Management from Ashford University.

As a best-selling author, motivational speaker, and soul stirring vocalist, Hudson's work has been featured on various platforms.

Her song "The Difference" has been released on spotify, tidal and apple music.

Shumon finds great joy in her roles as a mom, wife, and GiGi. She loves spending time with her family and close friends, cooking up delectable dishes to nourish their tummies, expressing herself through the pages of books that unlock truths within her heart, crafting music that soothes her soul and those around her, and providing thought-provoking motivation and inspiration to maintain balance within her life.

She is thankful for every hardship she has endured, having transformed her into the woman she is today. Through it all, she learned to trust in God and to have confidence in herself. She now lives in harmony in all facets of life, aspiring for excellence with every move she makes.

LAZAIRE BROWN JR

Lazaire Brown, Jr is a 26-year old Charlotte native who has always had a passion for helping others grow and develop. After graduating from West Mecklenburg High School as a Student Athlete with a certification in technology, he attended North Carolina A&T State University and graduated with his bachelor's degree in Graphic Communications. While attending school full time, Lazaire worked at Champs shoe stores and was awarded Number 1 Top Seller 2 years in a row.

He is now a dedicated member of Alpha Nu Chapter Kappa Alpha Psi Fraternity Inc., where he participates in the mission and purpose of the fraternity. Lazaire currently resides in Dallas, TX where he works as an assistant manager in the sales industry. He also hones his craft as a free-lance photographer capturing life's most cherished moments.

PRESTON BROWN

Preston Brown is a 22 year old young man with a bright future. Born and raised in Charlotte, NC, he graduated from West Mecklenburg High School with honors. There, he was a student and all star athlete, playing quarterback and taking the football program further in the playoffs than it had ever gone before. He was awarded All Conference Player in football and was crowned Homecoming King his Senior Year.

Preston was awarded multiple scholarships and began his secondary education at the University of North Carolina at Charlotte. After two years there as a student athlete, during which time he achieved Dean's List status, he is now attending Catawba College as a student athlete and continues to be on the Dean's List while pursuing his bachelor's degree in Communications with an anticipated graduation in December 2023.

This spring, he will be back on the football field as the quarterback. Preston enjoys playing football and looks forward to continuing his academic success.

SHUMAR BROWN

Shumar Brown is a 20-year-old Charlotte, NC native. He graduated from West Mecklenburg High School in 2020 and started his post-secondary education at North Carolina Central University before realizing it wasn't the right fit for him. Shumar is currently employed and determining his next steps.

A standout basketball player being awarded All Conference in his Senior Year of High School, Shumar enjoys playing competitively with friends whenever he can. He also has a passion for cooking, trying out new recipes and styles. In addition to that, he enjoys fashion and modeling and he takes the opportunity to be in front of the camera when possible. Always up for a good time, Shumar loves making people laugh and lives life on his own terms.

JAYSHAWN HUDSON

J ayshawn Hudson is a 26-year old man from Greenville, North Carolina. He moved to Charlotte, North Carolina in 2010 and graduated from West Mecklenburg High School as a Student Athlete. He continued his education at Livingstone College but determined that this was not the path he wanted to take. Jayshawn is currently working and being an amazing dad. He has a 3 year old son that he adores and takes great care of.

Jayshawn is also a musician in his own right with songs released under the name Moneyman Karti on Spotify, Apple Music, and Youtube Music. Jayshawn truly loves family and enjoys spending time with family as often as possible.